LOVE LETTERS FROM A YOUNG MAN

Antoinette de Morton

Published in Australia by Sid Harta Books & Print Pty Ltd,
ABN: 34632585293
23 Stirling Crescent, Glen Waverley, Victoria 3150 Australia
Telephone: +61 3 9560 9920, Facsimile: +61 3 9545 1742
E-mail: author@sidharta.com.au

First published in Australia 2023
This edition published 2023
Copyright © Antoinette de Morton 2023
Cover design, typesetting: WorkingType (www.workingtype.com.au)

The right of Antoinette de Morton to be identified as the Author of the Work has been asserted in accordance with the Copyright, Designs and Patents Act 1988.

All rights reserved. No part of this publication may be reproduced, stored in a retrieval system, or transmitted, in any form or by any means without the prior written permission of the publisher, nor be otherwise circulated in any form of binding or cover other than that in which it is published and without a similar condition being imposed on the subsequent purchaser.

Antoinette de Morton
Love Letters from a Young Man
ISBN: 978-1-922958-38-9 (paperback)
pp132

Dedicated to
Ahn Tuan

Date: Sunday 3 July 2005
Subject: I miss you too
To: Antoinette De Morton
From: Anh Tuan

My love I also ponder about you and asked my mum about you my mum really respect you she can not accept that I love you and one day if we have condition live together, but my mum till respect my affair reality I've met many girls but your heart and your mind different, I've been loving you when I decry (find out) that point I don't need some one special famous, I just need my girl is understanding me, can share for me everything of my mind, now I know I really love and need you I don't cry I don't crave (asking) your love, don't pretend (feign) or try show for you and any one else that I miss you, but I really miss you now, from bottom of my heart I love you. I become real man during the time I've met you, now I know I'm my heart right. I will write for you later. See you my love.

Date: Wednesday 6 July 2005
Subject: You OK, my love?
To: Antoinette De Morton
From: Anh Tuan

I'd spent one day for thinking (yesterday) any I've known that I've been really lucky when everything have come with me at the same time but conclusion since when I've met you everything but it's potential in my mind and body brisk and boom it's absolutely come with osmosis. The important thing is your fate and mine really matches (suitable) my father said like that. I've been feeling like that during the time we live together, I think you also thought like that, you know reality before I've influenced from Vietnamese culture so much but little by little it's changing especially when I met you I've think according to my heart every backward mostly gone I've looked for the nice culture of Vietnam and save it and do any things are good for the good people in there have my family and the important body is you, my love, I don't know when but it think about that, ponder. I don't know I'll exert myself more for do that but the short time I'm not sure can do something but I'll do by whole energy. I will say with Tim at once about that one your idea absolutely great I'm admirable so much I thirst for meeting you now my love, now I'm absolutely really strong in order to do anythings. Your children and husband OK? I now concern about them. See you soon. Kisses you.

Date: Thursday 7 July 2005
Subject: I happy again
To: Antoinette De Morton
From: Anh Tuan

Dear my love, I really happy when I receive your mails you alright it is wonderful, you try to explain for everybody about me is good, but if they're sceptic (doubt), it is ok because little by little they will understand, don't send me anything because it's not important, they will think no good. I love you. It is the truth I feel guilt if something is disadvantage for you. Don't think anythings, my love. I don't need someone emphathize for me if they don't want to do. So I've been talking with Tran (my friend) about you because I knew he was sceptic, I don't care he understand or not, but my affair, but your childrends they's different . they are love you very much if they think something about me just because of you they care of you, I respect that feeling, let's value it, no worries my love one day I will make they understand, now I think they've just been panic, who I am how my morals . don't do anything for me if it's make you difficult in behaviours with your folks, please even my flyer don't please don't if I do that I will feel really guilty . your folks important for you so much . we love each other in the heart, we will keep mailing it is ok, kisses you my love I don't know but now I'm exerting myself to do anything in order to improving my capacity for one day I will meet you again. Kisses my love . see you . Love Tuan

Date: Friday 8 July 2005
Subject: I'm waiting my love
To: Antoinette De Morton
From: Anh Tuan

My love, I'm waiting your coming but will not disappoint if the destiny can't bring you come . I think your husband , he's understand much more now, after chain of his decision about separate an go with other girl, he's more tolerant . it's good for him, because you always is good woman good wife, really sentiment, empathize with everybody, subtle ... I respect, value you so much I hope you have good life in future. I think it's will like that because the god not fair with you before now he must repay. I've been getting from you a lot of things, now I've been observing, believe in my will believe that if I try more is on day will have someone who was sent to me by the god to help me abut idea, way ... I love you more now because that point. I love you because my heart say like that I've so much emotion when I think about you I don't care anything because of I've been right so much reason in order to I know that you are so deserving to receive my love from me

I'm really love you from bottom of my heart, even I have no conception of love, but I know that the man really strong really believe in his capacity when have woman who understand his potential and enough intelligent come exchange feeling, soul ... and the guy will have special feeling reserve for her, I'm precious you, you like source of my strength, kisses you. Well, my love I think I should put the sentence: You will not be disappointed about us or your money back. Yesterday my relative send you the adjust one I miss one point is transport food drinks not included check I out for me please . See you thank you so much I will try out more ...

Date:	Saturday 9 July 2005
To:	Anh Tuan
From:	Antoinette De Morton

.... to why I have changed some language. I hope to get a job soon and am looking for something suitable.

I wonder if you could ask Tim a few questions for me?

1. What is the criteria for teaching Hanoi and does he think I could get work in January.
2. Who to ask regarding cheap flat or apartment when I come to Hanoi in December.

   If it is easier perhaps, he could give you his email address for me and I can discuss with him, if he does not mind of course. It is interesting I go to sleep thinking about you and Hanoi and wake up doing the same so you are very much in my thoughts so do not worry if emails don't arrive you will now that my computer is doing something dodgy. Much Love Antoinette

My sweet I am fine and think of you every day wondering how you are. I love receiving your emails they always put a big smile on my face I have definitely made up my mind to return to Hanoi at the end of December and will book a ticket soon. The pictures you sent are great and I will start work on a flyer this week. Please don't think that my time is ruined. I look forward very much to your emails and will keep them all (I am a hopeless romantic). I have not had any lovemaking since you and I now find it difficult to think of another man caressing me like you. The photos of the countryside weren't ruined so I will send tomorrow and send extra copies later. They are wonderful to have as I can see your face every day and remember out time together with much love and affection. I miss your tenderness and cuddles my love. Antoinette

My love are you alright, something are wrong. I really need to hear from you, even one word, I've been doing something wrong let's tell me. I'm sorry may be you busy, no worries my love I have no ideal now, please tell me, I miss you. I'm OK everythings of me OK. I'll wait, I hope nothing wrong, but let's tell me the truth I need it. I need you just you nothing else. Please tell me where are you ... Anh

Hi my love I am feeling much better today and my mind is busy thinking of ideas that can be implemented in Hanoi. I have spoken to my husband and he is willing to support me in any venture that I undertake and he is very happy that you are my friend and soulmate. I understand that Tran would be very sceptical of me but you can reassure him that I am honest and caring with you ulterior motives except to care for you and wish for your happiness. My children love me very much and also want for me to be happy no matter what the circumstances, my family understands that I have a strong connection to Hanoi and wish to return. Interestingly enough while I was in Hanoi so was Ian Findlay Brown the editor of the magazine that I showed you in the art gallery. He visited the gallery about two days after we had been and they told him that I had been there. It was a little disappointing that I did not know Ian was in Vietnam at the time.

If Cuong asks me to exhibit at the end of the year it would work out quite well as I could possibly ...
Antoinette

Date:	Monday 11 July 2005
Subject:	Where are you, tell me please
To:	Antoinette De Morton
From:	Anh Tuan

My love, are you alright, something are wrong, I really need to hear from you . even one work, I've been doing something wrong, let's tell me. I'm sorry may be you busy, no worries. My love I have no ideal now, please tell me I miss you, I'm ok everything of me ok, I'll wait, I hope nothing wrong, but let's tell me the truth I need it . I need you just you nothing else . please tell me where are you?

To: Anh Tuan
From: Antoinette De Morton

Hi my love, I am feeling much better today and my mind is busy thinking of ideas that can be implemented in Hanoi. I have spoken to my husband and he is willing to support me in any venture that I undertake and he is very happy that you are my friend and soulmate. I understand that Tran would be very sceptical of me, but you can reassure him that I am honest and caring with no ulterior motives except to care for you and wish for your happiness. My children love me very much and also want for me to be happy no matter what the circumstances, my family understand that I have a strong connection to Hanoi and wish to return. Interestingly enough while I was in Hanoi so was Ian Findlay Brown the editor of the magazine that I showed you in the art gallery. He visited the gallery about two days after we had been and they told him that I had been there.

It was a little disappointing that I did not know Ian was in Vietnam at the time.

If Cuong asks me to exhibit at the end of the year, it would work out quite well as I could possibly exhibiting in Hong Kong. I will wait and see what destiny brings. I have definitely made up my mind to return to Hanoi in December or there abouts depending on my finances which I am sorting out at present. Your flyer looks great, I will maybe suggest a couple of small changes and will email to you. I am picking up photos tomorrow so will send copies if they turn out next week. I look at your photograph and remember how cute you are and how much care for you. I miss your gentle caresses my love. Antoinette

---

To: Antoinette De Morton
From: Anh Tuan

My dear love, I really happy when I receive your mails you alright it is wonderful, you try to explain for everybody about me is good, but if they're sceptic (doubt), it is OK because little by little they will understood, don't send me anything because it's not important they will think not good, I love you. It is the truth I feel guilt if something is disadvantage for you, don't think anythings, my love. I don't need someone empathize for me if they don't want to do. So, I've been talking with tran (my friend) about you because I knew he was sceptic, I don't care he understand or not, but my affair, but your childrends they's different. They are love you very much if they think something about me just because of you they care of you, I respect that feeling let's value it, no worries my love one day I will make they understand, now I think they've just been panic, who I am how my morals, don't do anything for me if it's make you difficult in behaviours with your folks, please even my flyer, don't please don't if I do that I will feel really really guilty. Your folks important for you so much. We love each other in the heart, we will keep mailing it is OK, kisses you my love, I don't know but now I'm exerting myself to do anything in order to improving my capacity for one day I will meet you again. Kisses my love. See you. Love Tuan.

Date:	Tuesday 12 July 2005
Subject:	Hello my love
To:	Anh Tuan
From:	Antoinette De Morton

I am sending another email today, to you I hope you receive it. As said in last letter I am having problems with the computer. I have sent letter and photos to you today and you should receive in the next few days I have sent special post so somebody at your home will have to sign for it, so can you explain this will happen. I hope everything is okay with you.

    Much love Antoinette

Date:	Tuesday 12 July 2005
Subject:	Thanks God
To:	Antoinette De Morton
From:	Anh Tuan

My love I'm so happy when I hear from you, I'm sorry but I'd just been anxious, now everything ok. Today I still learnt English about tourism, my mind always tilling with your image your face wonderful it express that you are full vital, I think me so lucky now I'm really waiting December it will be great my love, I will finding the house when you come for us I know what to do, I wish your pictures about you come sooner. I will give Tim you propose as soon as possible (because he so busy). Kisses you, my love.

To: Antoinette De Morton
From: Anh Tuan

Hello my darling I have been sending emails everyday are you not receiving them below is last one sent. I have been having problems with my computer, the modem has been playing up, we have been trying to fix the problem, but have no idea what is going on. It could be that I need a new motherboard or something like that. I do not wish you to be upset of course I think about you every day. I have started rehearsals again for singing and will continue once a week it is fantastic and I hve a really good friend who is a sculpture and also musician so we practice quite a few songs this makes me very happy. I have sent photographs and a small something for you to remind you of me so please do not be offended as I have done this with much love. I will send copy of flyer soon with a few amendments and explanation as try my best, I, as a woman (gorgeous as that) thanks to you in some ways, I will have to still do some very hard things, e.g. give up my family home, the place my children grew up in etcetera etcetera (that is Latin by the way) and also my place of being for many years. We become comfortable and as human people it will always be hard to separate and become. I find now that my emails to you are becoming more detailed I hope this helps with your English and pronunciation, it is certainly helping me. I have never in my life spent so much time on a computer apart from working and doing database, files and all administrative bullshit. I write to you in these long hours and I find myself thinking of you. I am alone, not making any artwork obviously? Emailing to you. I think for the first time I am writing letters to my beloved but in a very direct way and using the computer for communication, this a first for me e.g. I have never done this before. Letter writing and ... my hair is soft like silken butterfly wings I imagine your caresses, also like silk soft, gentle when you need to be and hard when it is magnificent. You ae the beset and most beautiful man. My body is pale, round, and awaits your touch to be at one, music sings and I hear your soul and heart in my being, you my Adonis. Love Antoinette

... exhibiting in Hong Kong. I will wait and see what destiny brings, I have definitely made up my mind return to Hanoi in December or there abouts depending on my finances which I am sorting out at present. Your flyer looks great I will maybe suggest a couple of small changes and will email to you. I am picking up photos tomorrow so will send copies if they turn out next week. I look at your photographs and remember how cute you are and how much I care for you. I miss your gentle caresses my love Antoinette. Anh Tuan

Love Letters from a Young Man | Antoinette de Morton

Date: Thursday 14 July 2005
Subject: Thanks my love
To: Antoinette De Morton
From: Anh Tuan

My love I've been asking a few English school, the one said when you come here bring directly certificates, application to them, and your recording (CV) other said you send through emailing them your paper (the same last school) but I will be asking more but general you well enough capacity to apply job here let's trust me because I asked a lot of foreigner teacher most of them said so easy to ask job here because Vietnamese need talking with native speaker so much, more than that you are great better than them huge I'm not flirting, it's the true, my love, I feel really great when I said you are my girlfriend with thuan or some nice people you know that feeling make me happy a lot my love I love you from bottom of my heart, I'm waiting you every day. I'm learning hard every day in order to when you back we have beautiful time, I will come Ho Chi Minh when you come there, my love more and more I love you much much more. Kisses you, my love.

Date:	Sunday 17 July 2005
Subject:	My love
To:	Antoinette De Morton
From:	Anh Tuan

My love, I deeply believe in one things that we are were born for each other and I was born in order to endeavour because the most motivation the gods gave me is you I stick in that, I've know that I'm very lucky, my love I love you because I love you, I'll do anythings in order to you never sad or boredom about me, I'll do anythings any just blessing that you are happy and fun, my love never think anything I deeply love you from bottom of heart, now you are the most important for me, I'm waiting everyday kisses you, my love I love you so much, I want to cuddle you do anythings for love my love you are beautiful than very girl in the world now in my eyes I love you, let's send your pictures about you for me at once on emailing please I want to fondle you by kisses, kisses you my love.

Date:	Sunday 17 July 2005
To:	Anh Tuan
From:	Antoinette De Morton

It is late and I know I have just responded to your message but I want you to know that I deep in my heart and I can not explain this, that I miss you so much. I understand that there are many differences between us but when I even question these things it seems to matter very little, all I know is that you, my dear Tuan, will until, I see you again, remain always within my heart the dearest and most special love. Much love Antoinette

Date:	Monday 18 July 2005
Subject:	Kisses my love, I love you
To:	Antoinette De Morton
From:	Anh Tuan

My love, I'm home all day tomorrow to hear from you whenever you call, much love you, my love every day I always remind for my self I must do by somehow keep to have December I mean that, my love I'm the man but I can't call for my love in the birthday it's really mediocre and cowardly, but I promise with you that this problem won't happen again, I will do any things in order to make you never feel self-pity compare with every girl in the whole world. I love you my love, I promise that, I'm sorry because I can't do that at once but I'm the man I must and will kisses you much wish you have much fun, I love you, my love kisses you.

To: Anh Tuan

From: Antoinette De Morton

Hello my darling, I am well, I miss you too and I wish December will come quickly, life has become very busy here so the days pass by rapidly, I will be living at another place for next 2 weeks as I am house sitting for friends while they are on holiday, they have a computer so I will be able to email you every day. It is my birthday tomorrow and I am having a small party to celebrate, I am cooking all Vietnamese cuisine so I will be thinking of you, can you tell me that time you will be at home so I can telephone you,

I want to hear your voice. I hope the letter arrives in the next ay or so, it was only supposed to take 3 days and I sent it last Tuesday. Love and many kisses Antoinette.

To: Antoinette De Morton
From: Anh Tuan

My love, I deeply believe in one things that we are were born for each other any I was born in order to endeavour because the most motivation the gods gave me is you I stick in that, I've known that I'm very lucky, my love I love you because I love you, I'll do anythings in order to you never sad or boredom about me. I'll do anything any just blessing that you are happy and fun, my love never think ....

To: Anh Tuan
From: Antoinette De Morton

... and to leave my husband or get divorced. The husband does not care being he has his needs met without really having to do anything to make life better. It sounds like your father needs a good kick up the arse, but I suppose he will always that never change. It is the worst thing for a father to lose the res... wife and children though maybe your father does not know or even understand. Maybe he is disillusioned with the way his life has turned out and no longer can do anything too much including his family. He could also be depressed which affords capacity to see things clearly.

I don't know your mother manages, she is obviously an extraordinary woman able to deal with with all the situations that confront her, she must be very strong, I ... and soul and I admire her for her courage in adversity. My darling I hope you must be very frustrating for you to see these things happening in your family, must be very hurt and distressed to hear bad things about her son from his father hope this is not so. Your brother is at a very impressionable age and needs s..... that he does not mix with bad people and get into bad habits. Of course, I understand he thinks it is probably cool to try drugs and his friends probably try too. If he has no father to guide him with love and strength, then this is very sad. You will be a brother and father to him in someways, but not to tell him he is shit and no good otherwise he will feel more against family and try to rebel. Some of these think .....happened to friends of my daughter when their families hve broken apart and no support from the father and the mother left to manage with no money and struggle to raise children alone.

I am lucky my children are grown and are intelligent and so they understand the circumstances of their mother and father they love us both and we love them .... always proceed with events in the most caring way possible under the circumstances. Take care my darling. Much love Antoinette.

To: Antoinette De Morton
From: Anh Tuan

My love, you are alright, your ex-husband's really intolerant and selfish. I thought your decision is right, you know my mum can't do like you because her mind was occupied with so much caring and backward thinking my dad so bad, he has been so lazy, no responsibilities with his children and even his mum who always cared about him even she don't know how. It's never acceptable in Vietnam because if he don't care about his children it means his children may be get things from that society really easy because except family no body care about children but have many bad people make harmful for them because of Vietnamese they have narrow eyes they need so much money in short te.... And whatever in the future. So just my mum work all her lifetime with hard working in order to feed up for people on the other hand my that really sel..... he have no money almost of his lifetime so many times he took my mum's money away for buy things to smoke the more I grow up the more I recognise that he is so bullshit cowardly he so no responsibilities as far as he said my little brother smoke heroin with no sadness he just fabricate that story because of my mum take testify for him already but seem he want him smo.... That in order to my mum must regret because said him bullshit, oh dear, I hate him, my love you know the more I understand about that kind of people then I love and value you, kisses Antoinette, love you with the most fire I have.

To: Anh Tuan

From: Antoinette De Morton

I miss you too, so much, because we have bonded in our souls I will aways be there for you and care for you with my love. Life is full of many many surprises, it is what we make of situations that form who we become. There are many opportunities in life for love and joy yet many people miss these opportunities through fear, repression, conservatism and blindness. We are fortunate because we did not let a wonderful moment in life pass by, even though at the time I felt that it was perhaps not a good idea due to age differences etc. Because I listen to my heart I was able to be free to love you and not care about other people's prejudices and thoughts. I still do not listen when my husband calls me a fool and not facing reality, he speaks with a bitter tongue and I think the reality is that he is jealous but cannot admit to this. When I come to Ha Noi we will have a wonderful time and we will make a success of many things. Sometimes it takes more than one person accomplish many things and I have much drive and many thoughts of what can be done.

I am writing a lot and trying to become very clear in what is possible to achieve and what is realistic. Of course, I will have to be in Ha Noi to be able to gauge the possibilities. Only 4 and a bit months to go, I am sure this time will pass quickly though for I need time to sort out my circumstances here. I am having strong resistance from my husband who does not wish to sell the house and will make things difficult for me. I am strong and will be able to withstand his negativity. It is my life now and I plan to live a very full and exciting one. You are my love now Tuan and I long to see you and be near you. Antoinette

---

To: Antoinette De Morton
From: Anh Tuan

I miss you so much my love I don't know how to do but I know I love you so much respect you will so much and value you so much as well, I'll be waiting my love because I know in the whole universe just have only you understand me by heart by soul no girls in this world can do that so now I know if you leave me alone it means my life defeat mostly, I know that you will encourage me a lot of in my life before I'm really mediocre but when I've met you I have many ideas for improving myself reality I carry out pretty good and in depth of my heart my soul my mind I need you so much, I thirst for you. I like the ambitious fish always want to struggle with the life and you like the sea serious, I feel I can't live without you my love, I will hate my life if it is meaningless, I love you I need you my love kisses you, my love. Anh

---

To: Anh Tuan
From: Antoinette De Morton

I am very excited because I have found my home in another place. As I discussed with you I have my home with my husband and we still live together even though we are separated and do not have a marriage any more. Naturally this has been very distressing and I have in my own way have to come to terms with the disintegration of my marriage and trying to live in a civilized way with not too much angst or pain. I went for a wonderful dinner engagement tonight with an artist who has exhibitions in China and all around Australia. He has his property of 2 places on a big block of land and he wishes to sell one. We are in negotiation with this and possibly if I can reach an agreement with my husband, I can possibly think about this. I do not know if this is possible but will try my best I, as a woman (gorgeous as that) thanks to you in some ways, I will have to still do some very hard things, e.g. give up my family home, the place my children grew up in etcetera etcetera (that is Latin by the way) and also my place of being for many years. We become comfortable and as human people it will always be hard to separate and become. I find now that my emails to you are becoming more detailed, I hope this helps with your English and pronunciation. It is certainly helping me. I have never in my life spent so much time on a computer apart from working and doing a database, files and all administrative bullshit. I write to you in these long hours and I find myself thinking of you, I am alone, not making any artwork obviously?

Love Letters from a Young Man | Antoinette de Morton

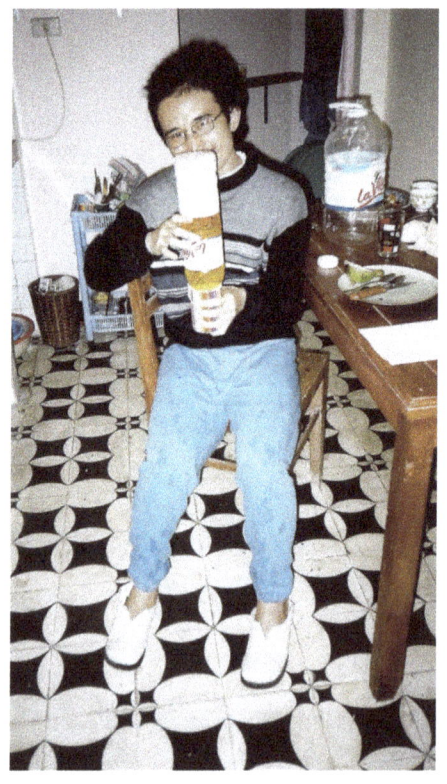

To: Antoinette De Morton
From: Anh Tuan

Hi my lovve the more I reading your email the more I love and miss you and understanding, I don't know what to say now but you know I miss your coming so much don't make shirts for me, I just say my love I'm so appreciate of this I love you I want to care of you cuddles you for understanding each other love you so much you know, please don't do that, I promise that you will proud of me from myself, I can't accept it please understand me, I'm really understanding your ideas when you want to make shirts for me I respect value that, now just only one thing I wish by whole heart is your coming here my love kisses Antoinette, Love you so much. Tuan.

To: Anh Tuan
From: Antoinette De Morton

My dear darling, the more I find out about you, becomes more interesting I bet you were so cute when you were a young child. Your mother has gone through many things for her family, more and more I respect her courage for standing her ground, believe me it takes an incredible woman to fight against the odds against her. In some ways I can relate to her struggle though I think in a male dominated society anywhere it is always difficult for women. I have been so busy seeing lawyers, real estate people etc. tat for the moment I little time for anything else. Everything is moving so quickly now that I hope I can keep up the pace. I am also being invited to many parties and social gatherings so things are hotting up. I am also being asked on many dates which seems really weird and somewhat confusing, it seems that now I am single, instead of being ignored which is what generally happens to women when they are separated from their husbands, the reverse is happening to me. I must be sending good vibes into the universe hey hey. Anyway, I am not thinking of such things though in some ways it is flattering. Basically, I am trying to get my life in order so I can come to Hanoi with a free spirit and no dramas. Unfortunately, my daughter is taking the situation very badly and is in tears at the breakdown of her family and the selling of her home. There is little I can do except be as supporting as possible especially as I am experiencing some grief too. I think the situation will become easier and I look forward to that time when we can all move on and get on with the rest of our lives. We have much to talk about when I come and I look forward so much to seeing you. Have my friend who is a fashion designer I am going to ask him to make some groovy tee shirts for you can tell me your size he will do this for me as a favour as he owes me. You will end up with something unique that no one will have in Vietnam. He is going to make some things for me also he is very good and very unusual he has dressed many famous models in the world. I have plans as I said and they include you, we will get something happening I am ever the optimist and I believe that we meet different people for different reasons even though we do not know why at the time. Even if things appear to be unusual like our situation there is meaning which may take a little time to unfold. Study hard my sweet and keep positive about life and the future, good things come to those with a good heart.

    Love and kisses Antoinette.

To:	Antoinette De Morton
From:	Anh Tuan

Hi my love, you know English now become my passion. It's only way I can contacting well to overseas, in order to can be doing something for the people who I love and owe them. The hard things it's not from language because I feel surely that I will achieve the top of English sills the hard things is myself, I need improve myself more and more and more .. but I think it's also no matter because I thirst for learning but I still must blessing and ask the god give me more power and lucky, the more I hear from you say about society it's the more I love and respect you and the more I understand that you're only person understands and will understanding me in my life the changing from me the developing from me maybe ins and outs ha ha …. and empathising me as well. I know that I'm so lucky, the god's given me angel, Antoinette, is that right my love. It's the truth I'm serious. Reality my childhood really bored, so cowardly afraid of every children the same age and more than, because I'd no opportunity to contacted to outside because my flat is secluded from outdoor and the gen from my dad and mum (not brave) and on the other hand my mum so busy with her business so her afraid me wander around to bad people so she locked the door when she went out, so much meeting made her so tired have about 4 meeting every weeks even Sunday the day which is only day teachers get break every weeks, they seem to want to kill my mum but fortunate my mum so touch she won in every meeting with clincher (still argue) for them she said she won because she was right, but I know she so clever every meeting every teachers are vote for president that she was right even the people who a few days ago is my mum's friends because they must care for themselves but my mum still empathetise for them, because they also have children they didn't want get sack, the result my mum lost after 3 years had fought but luckily at the same time my mum bought the flat near by there so even my mum lost but the price of property went up so my mum still enough money to established in Hanoi. You know I love you so much the more you want to understanding about my story the more I love and passion you. Kisses my love with my fire love Antoinette by whole heart. Tuan

To: Anh Tuan
From: Antoinette De Morton

Hello my sweet, it is wonderful to hear more about your history. Every family has a story to tell you more so with all the events that have taken place in your country and all the great changes. It is a sad think about power and the ability it has to corrupt the human spirit. These things happen here, there are many corrupt individuals who thrive on money and power at the expense of other people, luckily due to our system of democracy and free speech some of these powerful individuals get their comeuppance and fall from great heights metaphorically speaking. Unfortunately, there are those who do not get found out in their corrupt dealings and continue to wreak havoc on those less fortunate. Some politicians fall into this category as due those who own large chunks of the press and huge corporations who continue to destroy our planet and livelihoods with no care for consequences. The west has developed to some degree a high level of selfishness and a me me ideology, though not everybody thinks this way. There are many people in this country who are selflessness and do wonderful things for others that are less fortunate, these are the heroes that keep our belief in human integrity alive though they are not often rewarded as are pop stars, film stars etc. My life continues to be busy and I am trying to keep on top of everything, taxes, paperwork, letters, trying to organise the selling of my house, I think I need a holiday again ha ha. Occasionally my sense of humour deserts me and I get a little tense but I am working on that as well, I am very fortunate to have wonderful friends who give emotional support and keep from getting depressed. As I said the thought of coming back to Hanoi gives me something to look forward to and seeing you again. I am glad you are concentrating on your English, this is great it can only bring you benefits from hard work. It may not appear to others that you are working so hard, but I know how difficult this language is and the fact you are learning on your own behalf shows great fortitude and spirit and you can only win in the long run. I miss you heaps and think about you all the time. Much love Antoinette.

Date:	Sunday 20 July 2005
Subject:	I wish you were kissing me now
To:	Antoinette De Morton
From:	Anh Tuan

My love so much emotion from me now, I don't know how to describe, I love you, the love but you reserve to me so sweet and fire and kisses you, the poem you wrote about us have been showing exactly that we reserve for each other so much. Oh dear, I love you more than whenever your watch so nice I won't wear it but I've been sniffing the perfume from it, I put it on my pillow in order to remind that we are always together, your pictures in Paris (both of them) I kisses hem many time in your lip, it's made me crazy about my love, you look so cute and charming I love you when you called tour voice so sweet and beautiful it made my mind in seducing mad I had no idea, I love you, kisses you forever in the birthday, my love you don't send flyer for me just send through email it's easier don't send copies pictures for Thuan or Phuong when you come bring it, it's alright don't think anything. Kisses you, wish all of your wishes become real at least most of them. It's ok h h h.. kisses. My love.

Date:	Sunday 20 July 2005
Subject:	My dear sweetheart
To:	Anh Tuan
From:	Antoinette De Morton

Thank you for your beautiful thoughts about me, when I spoke to you I too had great emotions and I know how difficult it is to convey these emotions by telephone, when you are not near, the one that you care about. I wonder if I am foolish to consider your care for me, sometimes I feel silly and ridiculous to even consider that you could love me. I have great emotion for you too and much love and I wish that you were making love to me now. I feel your sweetness and light and I really miss your touch affection and love, you are my dear darling.

    All my love Antoinette.

Date:	21 July 2005
Subject:	I miss you
To:	Antoinette De Morton
From:	Anh Tuan

My love, I don't know what happen I can't contact to you, it like tricky from the god I don't know why my dad can't take to miss my book, I've been asking van Thuyet about your card but he said he busy. I'm sorry my love, I miss you so much worry about everything, how are you, you've been giving up smoking do you, I wish you take care for yourself good, you have good time in your birthday, your family care for you much, were they, you so cute, you know your image were embedded in y mind I miss your perfume, I sniff he beautiful smell in the ..? watch the money but seem the more I enjoy the more it's gone. Kisses you my love.

To:	Anh Tuan
From:	Antoinette De Morton

It is late and I know I have just responded to your

message but I want you to know that I deep in my heart and I cannot explain this, that I miss you so much. I understand that there are many differences between us but when I even question these things it seems to matter very little, all I know is that you my dear Tuan, will until, I see you again, remain always within my heart the dearest and most special love. Much love Antoinette

---

Date: 22 July 2005
Subject: I miss you
To: Anh Tuan
From: Antoinette De Morton

My love, I'll be waiting tomorrow kisses you so much, be frank, I love you by wi...? You in my most passionate I have, I love you. Kisses my love

Date:	22 July 2005
Subject:	Thanks god again
To:	Anh Tuan
From:	Antoinette De Morton

I miss you too my love I had a wonderful birthday celebration with lots of friends and family. I am not at my house at present I will be absent for another week, I will call you tomorrow afternoon. My number at home if 61 03 9 481 1041 or my mobile (03) 0417 440 480. It is funny, but I have my (previous) boyfriend and my husband chasing me but I only think of you now I think they are very jealous that we fo..... other so are behaving very strangely demanding my attention phoning constantly find out what I am up to. I am happy just to be alone at present with my thoughts, the desire to be back in Hanoi. I have seen Mai Ho and she will be in Hanoi in December/January, this will be good as she has many contacts and maybe available to assist you and I with contacts. If it were possible, I would be on a plane as soon as possible, but I have many things to work out here. I will speak to you tomorrow. Okay Antoinette

Date:	Saturday 23 July 2005
Subject:	My love, are you alright, I miss you so much
To:	Antoinette De Morton
From:	Anh Tuan

Haven't you received my mail yesterday yet, if you busy can't call for me don't ... when you have business, today I tried to call for you but it didn't gone thorough .. way of calling, I just may give you short calling, but I will have beautiful time enjoying the sweetness of your voice. I miss you so much today Thuan came to my home and I'd sl... pictures he said it so beautiful, he like you much, he understand that we love e... because of we get on perfect, my love today. I really the time as lengthen when contacting to you, my love I feel that your image imprint so deeply no-one can .. my love now I know I can't live without you, it's really heartfelt, I so love you I ca .. you don't come here in December, I'll do anything in order to you feel that I'm on your side, you are the girl but my heart have been overcoming very hard things you consider you ae the girl of my life let's trust me I'm really serious in this case .. much and I have decision that I will stick my heart at your trace kisses you, my love .....

Date:	Saturday 23 July 2005
Subject:	My love, are you alright, I miss you so much
To:	Anh Tuan
From:	Antoinette De Morton

My dear sweetheart, you love me because you have a beautiful heart and be.. shared the most special moment for you, you will always remember me because of this. It does not mean that you may find another love, you are a wonderful person and things change, as I have stated no matter what you will always be cherished, loved deep in my heart because our coming together was uniquely special to. I do not give my feelings lightly and will always be thinking of you and ways to ... I your life. I understand many things and the nature of the human heart, I will, no matter what be returning to Hanoi in December. All my love Antoinette.

Date:	22 July 2005
Subject:	I miss you
To:	Antoinette De Morton
From:	Anh Tuan

Hi my love, I'm afraid of I can't send email now I hope it's better, my love, I love you from the bottom of my heart, I don't know the concept of love but I'm well enough to say that I love you, I don't know how the love come, why it comes ... but I've just known that I'm falling in love with the girl but everybody think not right, they are stupid ridiculous crazy no body know about my feeling better than me, my nature was born in order to live in sincere love say, any things scratching from my deep of heart, my love now I love you more than ever, I don't know why but I really love you by whole heart, I have nothing but I have heart love you let's listen I love you seriously in my heart enough fire to burn anythings when I love you it become much much more after day by day, I love you kisses my love. Anh

Date:	Wednesday 20 July 2005
Subject:	My dear sweetheart
To:	Anh Tuan
From:	Antoinette De Morton

Thank you for your beautiful thoughts about me, when I spoke to you I too had great emotion and I know how difficult it is to convey these emotions by telephone, when you are not near, the one that you care about. I wonder if I am foolish to consider your care for me, sometimes I feel silly and ridiculous to even consider that you could love me. I have great emotion for you too and much love and I wish that you were making love to me now. I feel your sweetness and light and I really miss your touch affection and love, you are my dear darling. All my love Antoinette.

P.S. I wish you were kissing me now.

Date:	Sunday 24 July 2005
Subject:	Set your mind at rest to do anythings in your business, I love you so much
To:	Antoinette De Morton
From:	Anh Tuan

My love, I miss you so much I'm so happy when I knew you'll hve exhibiting your ... it's easier for you come Hanoi at that time, let's no worried about flyer, because ... scale hotel today, I think it'll go ok, I'll concentrate to work from now to when you ... nice more and more looking, it the more I descorve that you so cute, I think of action you've shown, it's the most motivation for me now, I'm so thirst for to be v... I'd sent message for you (maybe it's not gone through) from my cell-phone, me... maybe the last time my cosin sent mail he forget said the number of my cell-phone the way of using much some time I must ask some one help me to using, but n.... Love you.

To: Anh Tuan
From: Antoinette De Morton

My dear darling, I am so sorry I did not call you, I was expecting to be at my home ... changed. I got a gig in the countryside way out of Melbourne, plus I had a me ... director from Hong Kong. The good news is that I will be exhibiting my work in December or January which will work out perfectly with my schedule to be in Hanoi meeting to be in time to go to the gig which was several hours drive away, this email is so late as I hve only just arrived back at the house that I am looking at my house at all today which is the only place I can telephone you. I will do so not telephone from here as it would be discourteous. I am very happy thinking Greek sculpture by the way of a perfect young man which comes from Greek moral support with my idea to be in Hani all my really good friends think it is ...

   Much love Antoinette

To: Antoinette De Morton
From: Anh Tuan

Have you received my mail yesterday yet, if you busy can't call for me don't want ... you have business, today I tried to call for you, but it haven't gone through, calling, I just may give you short calling but I will have beautiful time enjoy ..... voice. I miss you so much today Thuan came my home and I'd shown for h..... it so beautiful, he like you much, he understand that we love each other be perfect, my love today, I really the time as lengthen when I can' contacting that your image imprint so deeply no-one can't throw it out, my love now I ... you, it's really heartfelt, I so love you I can't withstand if you don't come here any things in order to you feel that I'm authentic man in your side, you are ... have been overcoming very hard things in order to love you consider you a ... let's trust me I'm really serious in this case I'm ponder so much and I have ... my heart at your trace kisses you, my love.

To: Anh Tuan
From: Antoinette De Morton

My dear sweetheart, you love me because you have a beautiful heart and shared the most special moment for you, you will always remember me because it does not mean that you may not find another love, you are a wonderful change, as I have stated no matter what you will always be cherished and my heart because our coming together was uniquely special for me also ... feelings lightly and will always be thinking of you and ways to help you in understand many things and the nature of the human heart, I will no matter what be returning to Hanoi in December. All my love Antoinette

To: Antoinette De Morton
From: Anh Tuan

Hi my love, I'm afraid of I can't send email now I hope it's better, my love .. you from bottom of my heart, I don't know the concept of love, but I am willing enough to say that I love you, I don't know how the love come, why it comes .. I've just known that I'm falling in love with the girl but everybody think now they are stupid ridiculous crazy nobody know about my feeling better t... my nature was born in order to live in sincere love say, anythings scra... from my deep of heart, my love now I love you more than ever, I don't know why but I really love you by whole heart, I have nothing but I have hear... you let's listen I love you seriously, in my heart enough fire to burn anything when I love you it become much much more after day by day, I love you my love

---

Date: Tuesday 26 July 2005
Subject: Hello my love
To: Antoinette De Morton
From: Anh Tuan

Thanks love so much about calling and flyer, I love you more and more I know it's destiny but I thrust for to be together with you, I always blessing the god every days let's bring her to me, please I know it's will work, I love you in my lifetime I don't know why but in my thinking you are definitely

get considering that you are my girl my woman of mine, I've contacted with many girl and I have great woman to consult for me a bout girl of mans' life is my mum but you are beautiful woman who I can't find anywhere else, I love you.

To:		Anh Tuan
From:		Antoinette De Morton

It was wonderful to hear your voice today, you sound as cute as ever, I have gone the flyer and will email it to you tomorrow hopefully. I will also email to address you provided. Thinking of you, much love Antoinette

---

Date:		Tuesday 26 July 2005
Subject:	In my chemise
To:		Antoinette De Morton
From:		Anh Tuan

My love I understand your thoughts, it's from my feeling, I love you by whole heart I need just you (your body your soul your spirit) and nothings else, from bottom of my heart, I want to say that I need you than anythings in the whole world, now I've been making decision for myself, I pay that my love let's come here please, now, I really beseech you please come here in the end of this year I'm swearing destiny if you can't come, when you come I'll take you come any places but we'll have good life, oath anybody in the whole world don't know any things about the love, feeling just just have only one fucking bloody things to do is nosy in other peoples' business but I crave you that let's don't care about that, please ok, I love you that's all I just think about our life when you come we will live together make business together .. I've considered you life my wife already. We'll watch over you care of each other just live for each other, and I want to say again I just need only yourself nothings else from you I'll work do anything for your life. Kisses you my love, I love you so much, now I'm serious than whenever I love you

To:	Anh Tuan
From:	Antoinette De Morton

In my white chemise I think of you and your lovemaking I wish now that you were within me it is you my love that I think of from now on. I wish that only you were giving me your love and your penis I think only of you my Adonis. I find now it very difficult to understand any other man, even though I am desired now, with boyfriend ringing I find myself indifferent.

 I am now without husband who also desires me. I remain myself and even through every aspect of consideration I consider myself different I will always remain a magnificent woman worthy of your affection and love. Antoinette

Date:	Wednesday 27 July 2005
Subject:	My love
To:	Antoinette De Morton
From:	Anh Tuan

My love, I've just waken up but your image in my brain say I must came here to waiting my love, your picture very mice, I kisses in there many times it remind me about you I become crazy when I can't get sex and touching you fondle you so frustrating all nights I couldn't sleep well, had waken up many times looked at your pictures especially the night before you calling I love you so much, your gesture you cute when you point and ha ha, when you tried to pretend saying making harm with supper glue, oh dear I love it I love every movement of you, it so so cute I'm so lust now, oh dear I love you, my love kisses you for meet my derise but seem it's not enough I need touching, I love you, kisses you. My love don't send copies of flyer for me, thanks my love, love you Tuan

---

To: Anh Tuan
From: Antoinette De Morton

I am glad that you understand me, perhaps you more than anyone else know my heart and soul, do not worry I will definitely be in Hanoi at the end of December no matter what even if I have to beg borrow or steal (that is a joke ha ha) I have emailed you the flyer for your perusal and have also emailed to the guy that you helped when his wallet was stolen. I will make copies of the flyer and give to travel agencies around Melbourne and also make copies and send to you if you like. I have changed some of the language in the flyer as "bad" could seem negative and also "cheap transport" could come across as makeshift or faulty transport. I hope that these changes are acceptable let me know and I will distribute flyers as soon as possible. I miss you and love you Antoinette

Date:	Thursday 28 July 2005
Subject:	My love
To:	Antoinette De Morton
From:	Anh Tuan

My love, how are you, every things are good aren't they, I know you're busy don't worry about emailing for me, some time it's ok we will have good time when you come, today Tim called for me and said "tell with Antoinette that wage or salary for teaching

English is really good, don't worry about that I can earn 1500 USD for month with having lesson every afternoon per lesson 1.5 hour.." may be he must work more but he said it's very comfortable. I miss you so much. I'm always waiting to the end of this year, with no matter what that I will work enough for myself in order to we live well together, I miss your gestures and actions so much, I love you, kisses you, my love.

To: Anh Tuan
From: Antoinette De Morton

I am glad that you understand me, perhaps you more than anyone else know my heart and soul, do not worry I will definitely be in Hanoi at the end of December no matter what even if I have to beg, borrow or steal (that is a joke ha ha) I have emailed you he flyer for your perusal and have also emailed to the guy that you helped when his wallet was stolen. I will make copies of the flyer and give to travel agencies around Melbourne and also make copies and send to you if you like. I have changed some of the language in the flyer as "bad" could seem negative and also "cheap transport" could come across as makeshift or faulty transport. I hope that these changes are acceptable, let me know and I will distribute flyers as soon as possible. I miss you and love you. Antoinette.

Date:	Friday 29 July 2005
Subject:	My dear sweetheart
To:	Antoinette De Morton
From:	Anh Tuan

My love don't worry I've been understanding you, because you are my love, we amply emotional, it's one of the some mainly reason but I love you, everything you've been expression is, really right it's authentic your heart, you are one of the best the world hve emotion, feeling beautiful like that, I love you and I know not on body hve had condition contacting with you also love you to, I'm proud of that in emotional and kisses you in passionate of love .. I love you so much, my love

Love Letters from a Young Man | Antoinette de Morton

Love Letters from a Young Man | Antoinette de Morton

To: Anh Tuan
From: Antoinette De Morton

Forgive me for not emailing you yesterday. I have had much sadness, unfortunately dear and sweet man who was the husband of one of dearest friends died, he was Balinese from Indonesia and he was not an old man, he has left his wife, my 2 very young children, naturally I am in shock and heart sad, I cannot say how I feel about this situation, enough to write that I have had too many gins and to needless to (say) write (I am totally off my trolley so to speak) ask Tim about .. will explain. I miss you now more than I can say, I am lucky though I have many and dear friends who are being wonderful and supporting at this time, I can and get used to death emotionally, I have seen and witnessed too many lately, many musicians who keep (dropping dead like flies) another Tim question for you, I explain. I think of you my dear Adonis. All my love Antoinette.

Date:	Sunday 31 July 2005
Subject:	My dear sweetheart
To:	Anh Tuan
From:	Antoinette De Morton

I am good, I hope you enjoyed time in the countryside, it is always good for the spirit to be near nature and not always in the city and I hope your mum enjoyed as well as that you were visiting for pleasure and not for any sad reason. I have not been to Laos, but I have met people who have and they say it is a wonderful place with many beautiful temples. Did you hear about the job in the hotel? Not that it really matters as I think things occur when they are meant to and if this is not the right job there will be something that sits your soul. As I said I am busy painting and very occupied my social life has calmed down and I feel content just to make paintings and write and think of you my love. I am counting the months till December. All my love Antoinette

To:		Antoinette De Morton
From:	Anh Tuan

Hi my love, I'm really happy when you alright, I was must took my mum come back my mum's countryside in 2 days it's definitely crazy because of it has no internet-stores at all. I love you so much and miss you my love, when you come we will discuss about go to Lao (have you been there) seem I like it so much I'd had condition to contacted with Laos people they very nice and a lot of foreigners also said it's very nice, as well, if you like do that we will have a lot of fun I'm understanding your thinking by my heart, I love you blessing your action is always right but I'm sure they are always reasonable. Much love my love Tuan, kisses my love.

To:		Anh Tuan
From:	Antoinette De Morton

I hope you are well, I am now back in my house and trying to get back to normal. It has been very unusual living by myself but it has certainly strengthened my resolve to change my circumstances, for example selling the house and totally leaving my husband. I don't know how long this will take but will probably be some time next year. I am painting again and am continuing having rehearsals and learning new songs. I have printed off all the emails that you have sent and look at them again with much love as they are like a kind of diary that continues each day. I will save these in a special album for my family so that they will understand in the future, part of my history. Maurice continues to see his girlfriend and I think they are very happy, he is not at this house very much these days but we continue to be friends and talk about each other's lives and the direction such things will take. I would like to organise my ticket as soon as possible but I have to wait to hear what is going to happen in Hong Kong as it would be easier to coincide me coming to Hanoi and the exhibition. This may not work but I will take events as they occur and continue to look forward to being in Hanoi at the end of December. I miss you and your cuddles and think of you always. Much love Antoinette.

Date: Sunday 7 August 2005
Subject: Hello my love
To: Antoinette De Morton
From: Anh Tuan

Hi my love, I'm ok, I'd been trying to use my cosin computer during the time till now but it's been so hard to access, my cosin really nice when he knew I need to access internet he's tried to help me and said to me that I can come his home use his facilities for learning I'm so appreciate that and I'll try to help him learning English improving his English skill, when you come I will definitely recommend him to you really good man honest may be he can't understanding many things but he's really good guy. I miss you so much I'd called for him many time, but it's not work (the computer) I'm so angry because he forgot to give me the keys of his house twice times during the time he was working in countryside now I've been coming back home it's better I've just borrowed his radio any books. That's ok my mind always appear your image, your gesture your action, your smiling I can't describe but the love I've reserved for you more and more grow up bigger. Antoinette I love you so much.

Date: Monday 8 August 2005
Subject: Hello my sweet
To: Antoinette De Morton
From: Anh Tuan

Hey my love I've been feeling much better when I hear your voice, the calling is wonderful but ironically it's costed a lot of money I know you can be competent but anyway having money now is the best way because you … will pens a lot of money when you come to Vietnam in December of this year, I will try to reduce it, thanks my love so much about the calling you are beautiful girl in the whole world but I know so tolerant, mercy, empathetise with many range of people even the people have done bad things for you I so proud of you and I understands why you do that it's also the reason but we're falling in love each other, my love you so much, you've made my life better a lot I can't not say anythings now but I love and thirst for you, kisses my love.

To: Anh Tuan
From: Antoinette De Morton

I hope everything is ok with you and your family. Everything is good here I have been kept very busy painting. It is still freezing cold so I have to keep the fire burning all the time because the house gets so cold there are too many rooms to keep warm. My studio is outside so I have to wear many layers of clothing to keep warm and my hands freeze so sometimes it is hard to use my paint brushes. I certainly miss the warmth of Hanoi though I know it can get cold there too. I will telephone in the next few days if you let me know when you are home. How is your English progressing are you still chatting to tourists at bi hoi? Say hello to Hien for me if you still go to that bia hoi. Also if you get a chance can you pop into Classic 2 hotel and find out how Min Min (kitty) is going and if she is still alive and growing, and tell them I will be back late December and hope to see her big and fat ha ha. Missing you heaps, much love Antoinette.

To:	Antoinette De Morton
From:	Anh Tuan

…. don't know it's good or not good but will try out, I'll work in effort. I'll make sure with him that when you come I'll get long vacation, don't worried he needs me. I thurst for my vacation at that time, my love I miss you so much I will work hard till there I've known you've done already, good luck my love thanks your picture so much it help me things positive in this time, my mum like countryside so much but she came there for her business, any way she had good time there. I will work in 20th of this month so that time good for me cultivating my English. Kisses you a lot, I love you, wish all the best for you.

To:	Anh Tuan
From:	Antoinette De Morton

I am good, I hope you enjoyed time in the countryside, it is always good for the spirit to be near nature and not always in the city and I hope your mum enjoyed as well and that you were visiting for pleasure and not for any sad reason. I have not been to Laos but I have met many people who have and they say it is a wonderful place with many beautiful temples. Did you hear abut the job in the hotel? not that it really matters as I think things occur when they are meant to and if this is not the right job there will be something that suits your soul. As I said I am busy painting and very occupied by social life has calmed down and I feel content just to make paintings and write and think of you my love. I am counting the months til December. All my love Antoinette.

To: Antoinette De Morton
From: Anh Tuan

My love you know I also thirst for touch your body fondle you kisses your body I'm so lust now I thirst for you. Thirst for make orgasm my love much more than whenever I want to get sex with you I'm waiting your coming I blessing every day, I want make sure with the god that you will come. I hope you can call me tomorrow morning 8.8.2005 I'm loving and waiting your phone if you can't phone no worries I'll waiting next day in the morning. Kisses you my love, I love you.

To: Anh Tuan
From: Antoinette De Morton

Hello my darling, I miss you and am thinking of you. I am trying to be normal in my culture and working and maintaining and maintaining credibility, ha ha. I am still a woman and artist here and things are very interesting regarding me being a so called single and now not being with my husband. Since the death of my dear friend I hve felt a little disillusioned with some things, my heart feels strong but my soul misses you and of course my body misses you. I, like you, have not been the same since. It is very hard for me to be here and think of you without being emotional and rational and then wonder how we can be. I love you and miss you with all my heart and yet feel silly for feeling this way. My dear darling all I want is this minute to be with you to feel your cuddles you within me your beautiful eyes gazing at me when you love me. Love and much love Antoinette

To:	Antoinette De Morton
From:	Anh Tuan

My love, I'm sorry because I'd had emailing for you, I'm so frustrating, are you alright everythings alright I couldn't get job in the hotel but that guy who recommended me to that hotel said will keep me work for him has done fabrics furniture he's Singapore he get married with Vietnamese girl, so he will stay in Vietnam long time, speak perfect Vietnamese, he said I will do operator or write quote a price in computer or distribute goods, I .....

Date:	Tuesday 9 August 2005
Subject:	My love, I thirst for you so much
To:	Antoinette De Morton
From:	Anh Tuan

Hi my love I lust for you so much, I'm really keen to cuddles you take off your clothes kisses your body push my penis in hug you with active action listening when you heave sound with pleasure you have, we fondle each other enjoy the best orgasm we have whenever I remember at moment you said push in I'm so crazy your voice so beautiful strong but gentle I love you so much my love I'm waiting and will waiting to the end of this year. I love when remember the time we had in June I enjoy it so much but seem the more I enjoy it also is the more I thirst for your coming my love, I really miss you so much touching you gazing enjoy your feelings. My love kisses you love you so much. Tuan

---

To: Anh Tuan

From: Antoinette De Morton

I loved hearing your voice today, though I think I talk too much and you say not so much, I know it is difficult communicating via the telephone, I have never really liked this way of speaking myself. I did know at the time that Classic 2 hotel ripped me off but I like to do things with good grace. Many backpackers will never return so they do not care about saving face. Because I knew I would be returning I can speak and say truthfully, that upon my return that I am not happy with the rip off and still remain friendly and have dignity. Deborah and Susan will never return to Classic 2 hotel so it did not matter to them if they caused a fuss it will always be only another story to them. Naturally, I understand that the people who work in Classic 2 Hotel have to get money as the best they can, they also live and work in Hanoi and I do not. I am to them a transient traveller whom they think they will never see again and that they can make money from me because I cause no argument I do not feel anger about this it is the way of travelling, I know that many people in Hanoi automatically think that all westerners have lots of money, unlike me who travels always by the skin of my .....

Date: Thursday 11 August 2005
Subject: Hello my darling
To: Antoinette De Morton
From: Anh Tuan

My love how are you I guess you are busy with your works, it's very good I miss you so much I just think of you, you so charming when you make kidding it's the image but it's appearing now in my mind, I love your dark side when it's appeared when you pretended make harm by super glue when you were laughing some one who land in deep shit so funny so cute my love your heart so young nothing old at all I like the way you said I was flirting you when we had been sitting in the bar has good view to the lake seem you were sceptical you know at that moment I really wanted to eating you, you always very lovely and charming in my eyes my love kisses you love you so much. Tuan

---

To: Anh Tuan
From: Antoinette De Morton

My love you nearly give me orgasm just reading your email I love and miss you terribly and think all he time of your love making, nothing compares to you my darling it is strange the longer I do not see you and the more we email each other the harder it becomes for me to be apart, I feel almost like a teenager when I think of you my heart races and I long to feel your lips pressed upon mine and your beautiful body close and inside. If I could I would fly tomorrow but this is not to be but I am working on things so maybe a miracle will happen (I still believe in miracles) and my situation will alter dramatically. You will always be in my heart my love Antoinette

---

Date: Friday 12 August 2005
Subject: Hello my darling
To: Antoinette De Morton
From: Anh Tuan

Hi my love I love you by many reason but seem I've been passionate with no reason my love, frankly I thought the original love perfect because of it's so pure .. It's so pure so the bull shit people never know because in their eyes and brains get busy so much from mediocre life, the love so beautiful because the pulsing (vibration) of heart so natural the feeling from each body and the understanding from soul, I love you with much the intangibility passionate I can't explain about it, just think that I passion every your movement your gesture you …. Thought my love I know you understand that so much so it's reason I'm love you more and value you more and more. I know that in stupid life like now in this world no body pure like you but I can get my love you so valuable toward me you know, kisses you I'm really love and thirst for you my love kisses you Tuan

---

To: Anh Tuan
From: Antoinette De Morton

Hello again my sweet, I love the way you remember particular moments!!! Believe me when I asked if you were flirting with me I have to admit I was very nonplussed. I was not sceptical, "just this is ridiculous", at the time I felt something but I did not know. We were friends as far as I knew at that particular moment, though there was something in our eyes that made me think ah ha! So naturally I was a bit bemused by the circumstance of that occasion. I would have never thought then that you considered me in a lustful way but I am so glad that you do and have considered me so. I would have never have been so forward, if you had not expressed your desire I would have not thought that this would be so. I still feel a little strange that even this could be so, but I am an emotional and caring being and love you so what the "hell" as they say. I believe that things happen for a reason and that sometimes it is best not to think or analyse too much (I need to take my own advice sometimes). I am thinking of you and my body and mind thirsts for you also, my dear darling everything will be fine I know this in my soul. Antoinette

---

Date: Sunday 14 August 2005
Subject: Hello my darling
To: Antoinette De Morton
From: Anh Tuan

Hi my love I'm really happy when you have nice time with your daughter and he birthday you are beautiful woman (and girls in my eyes) I'm not really surprise to close to you because you always listening from young people's idea and want new idea (of course it's positive things) I love every things from you your husband, his interfering (nosy) seem I love you more when you pissed frankly, my love much reality I thirst for your coming I want to ignore (don't care little bit but I can .. also pissed as well Tim took my to swanky night club actually I'm not really enjoying .. expensive but Tim is really nice he wanted me came there and he always asked around there and checked that I love you or not really I value him about that point always waiting for your coming we will have big party when you come, I know do… important things is not easy but you thought careful do it, is really good even your things but, nothing perfect, so let's stronger but you must balance really careful you my love about every things I thought really careful about us for long run and definitely never regret about my decision I love you we will live together forever will do any thing for us will not lazy like some Vietnamese man will become good …. Lean to kisses you my love Tuan love Antoinette so much.

Date:	Sunday 14 August 2005
Subject:	My love
To:	Antoinette De Morton
From:	Anh Tuan

My love the more I reading your emails is the more I find our souls attaching and intermingle as one and the more I finding I cant lose you in my life I love you my love I love you because your soul your hear so pristin (pure) your characteristic I understand that it's all for the girl, woman of my life I love you and need you for my life I'm in earnest. I know you understand me Antoinette. I'm really serious this moment and say Antoinette, I love you and one stick at you in my life time I just need you and nothing else, now I have nothing with money or property and I'm stinking hate use your money or your possession but I have will and resolution and heart love you, value you so much I will do every thing for us if you go with me. I'm waiting to the end of this year in order to you challenge. I know you understand but I want make sure that I will do anything for us. Love Antoinette, Tuan kisses.

To: Anh Tuan
From: Antoinette De Morton

I loved hearing your voice today, though I think I talk too much and you say not so much, I know it is difficult communicating via the telephone. I have never really liked this way of speaking myself. I did know at the time that classic 2 hotel ripped me off but I like to do things with good grace. Many backpackers will never return so they do not care about saving face. Because I knew I would be returning I can speak and say truthfully, that upon my return that I am not happy with the rip off ad still remain friendly and have dignity. Deborah and Susan will never return to Classic 2 hotel so it did not matter to them if they caused a fuss it will always be only another story to them. Naturally, I understand that the people who work in Classic 2 Hotel have to get money as the best they can, they also live and work in Hanoi and I do not. I am to them a transient traveller whom they think they will never see again and that they can make money from me because I ...

My dear darling I have come back from the big party, I have danced and had a good time. It is now late, but I feel alive from wonderful experiences and beautiful young women and men. I have been embraced as friend and loved and feel really s... not know how much my daughter's friends loved me so much. They kept asking to dance and share laughter and fun, memories and beauty and many many hugs and kisses. I feel so privileged to have been in this very happy situation. You say I have a young heart, I think you are right, tonight in some ways was testimony to my ability to connect with people young and older, my dear darling daughter and friends talked, as did I for my daughter on her special day. Oh! It was so w.... to be a part of so much. I am home now, and they are all getting thoroughly (pissed .. drunk). My husband (ex) left early as always and when he says bad things to me ... (if you Tuan really knew me) e.g. If I ever get drunk that you would not care for me, this is his point of view. As I said we became friends first and I was not seeking flattery or love. So, my views and outspokenness had nothing to hide or nothing to gain so I was and am to you. I will and not ever be the cause of untruthfulness is (I hope, my father died from his 4th heart attack at 55 .....) and full of love, always it remembers beauty, you and the gift of gods and the universe. Love is a special and fabulous thing and even though I my have mis ... I cherish and will never deny, no matter how hard here, and in my circumstances people saying (are you joking). You are and will always be my dear darling and for your touch and miss you, you are not near me, I too kiss your photograph and are near your cute gaze, your seriousness, your intensity, I will never forget you the sharing of your and my view of the lake (remember I have the photograph sitting at the table) my darling Tuan you will always be in my heart and mind an ... All my love Antoinette

---

Date: Monday 15 August 2005
Subject: My dear darling
To: Anh Tuan
From: Antoinette De Morton

Oh my love I am thinking of you constantly and feel very sad that I cannot be with you when I am going through this turbulent time. My house is chaos with boxes every half finished packing. I can not think straight about the future until I have and sett... I miss so much your cuddles and lovemaking and cooking together everything. Anh you are the one for me and I wish I could do something right away but things will take ... try very hard to come back to see you. All my love and kisses my darling Antoinette

Hi love to day I got up bit earlier than the other days I miss so much the feeling and sleep ad I cuddle you eave the bed for awhile and back again cuddle you stroke your breasts you waiting for your waking up and after that is great m... sexual time love I miss you like crazy love you so much kisses love Tuah.

Kisses to you and all my love my sweet, I am going crazy without your love, I'm bereft without you, love Antoinette

Hi love thanks for the call I'm really crazy about not talking to you such a long time I feel totally good now waiting for your call. Kisses love Tuan

I got your message on my mobile and I will call you tomorrow Thursday around 12pm midday your time. I have been looking into the voicemail thing and a friend of mine said I can get voicemail and webcam. I have been so busy packing that the days are running away from me and there is still so much to do. Some days I wake up and think oh my god this is horrendous but I have to continue. It is probably not worthwhile for me to set anything up here as I will be gone in a couple of weeks so when I get my computer organized in the new house I will set things up. Though I will give it a go on Yahoo and see what happens hey. I miss you so much too that I have been very flat, I will do my best to come back to Hanoi as soon as I am able. I will call you tomorrow. All my love Antoinette

Antoinette you know that how much I want you next to me.

It is impossible for me to come there with you I'm fucking frustrating about that and I know some time I've been blind because of jealous now I try to ignore things less think about rabish but the more I think about you the more I be crazy and stupid but no worries I've known you are really busy now I might so unreasonable but love why you don't call me I really run out of money or tried to access the programme in internet is skype.com and make your vocal email address mine is "hoanganhtuan 1983" I hope to do it in there easier than in Vietnam wish to talk to you soon kisses. Love Tuan

My dear darling you are becoming fluent ha ha

in English. ha ha. and with oh my god orgasm, I so wish I wish I was with you yesterday and today of course. I am pleased you are back in Hanoi, this is where we met and our destiny. I am not sure why as yet but deep in my soul I know this to be true. Every time I look at our photograph together I see beauty, heart and soul. Ours together, all my friends now comment on the happiness we seem to shar and how happy and beautiful I look in your company my dear love. How things change ha ha. I would give anything now to be with you, my brain is working overtime to think of a way to come back to Hanoi. All I am doing at present is packing more pacing and packing and now you understand the meaning of bereft a little of that too. My dear darling I cannot say in words how much you mean to me, I miss you and love you and wish so much I was with your, especially your fabulous fucking your sucking of my breasts your touching my whole body god I miss you, now I will have to have … my darling I will think of you, All my love. Antoinette

Hi love I miss you so much I've just messaged for you to ask you call for me but I thought you are busy Tim will teach me some English with his student it's really great I will try the best to comprehend. Kisses love Tuan

It is late at night again here for me, you are not with me so my sleep is nothing you are not.

Date: Tuesday 16 August 2005
Subject: My dear darling
To: Antoinette De Morton
From: Anh Tuan

My love you do nothings burden me I feel uncomfortable if you thought like that, between us have no obstacle, I feel better when you tell me the stories I value the things which you tell me like that when you come I'll make you feel comfortable and happy with the best I have, you will never feel not well with the tie we have in near future, I love you and I understand that love will conquer all so now I have much confident that I will become good man of your my love, you know the more ignorant people judgement about us is the more I love you and value you my love, I thirst for get sex with you, get orgasms for each other, caresses you kisses you with the most passionate, I can't describe the fire emotion now my love I just say that I love you thirst for you so much. Kisses you Antoinette, love Antoinette Tuan.

To: Anh Tuan
From: Antoinette De Morton

I am writing again to you, because I want to and I miss you and I am really grumpy with my ex-husband. He is being most unreasonable which I thought he might be. Now I want things to move on he is becoming obstreperous (e.g. grumpy) and having sex with me at the same time. As I say no he is even more grumpy. I know he is trying to fix things in his own way, but it is becoming increasingly uncomfortable for me to live in the same house. Now that I have established my desire to move the family are becoming quite disconcerted as I guess they thought that things would improve and that we would get back together (my husband and I). Life is a funny thing I know in my heart what I want to do and can do so and yet there will always be obstacles in doing so. Of course, these obstacles are not insurmountable and no matter what I will be in Hanoi at the end of December, though I have heard because of Tet prices may be more expensive. I am planning to see the travel agent this week and negotiate the best deal. I do not wish to burden you with some unpleasant aspects of my life, but I feel that you need to know some of these things. All ....

Date: Wednesday 17 August 2005
Subject: My dear darling
To: Antoinette De Morton
From: Anh Tuan

My love you are alright, your ex-husband's really intolerant and selfish, I thought your decision is right. You know my mum can't do like you because her mind was occupied with so much caring and backward thinking my dad is so bad he's been so lazy no responsibilities with his children and even his mum who always cares about him even she don't know how. It's never acceptable in Vietnam because if he don't care about his children it mean his children may be get bad things from that society really easy because except family no body care about children but have many bad people make harmful for them because of Vietnamese they have narrow eyes they need so much money in short term and whatever in the future, so jut my mum work all her lifetime with hard working in order to feed up for people on the other hand y that really selfish we have know money almost of his lifetime so many time he took my mum's money away for buy things to smoke the more I grow up the more I recognize that he is so bull shit cowardly he so no responsibilities as far as he said my little brother smoke heroin with no sadness he just fabricate that story because of my mum take testify for him already but seem he want him smoke that in order to my mum must regret because said him bull shit oh dear I hate him, my love you know the more I understand about that kind of people the more I love and value you, kisses Antoinette love you with the most fire I have.

Date:	Thursday 18 August 2005
Subject:	My dear darling
To:	Antoinette De Morton
From:	Anh Tuan

My love thanks so much about advice and sharing the way of your telling really brother not smoke any narcotics except cigarettes so far, my mum will put him for help .. in order to help him take practical because my mum think if have some things to .. him, I've been taking with him many times and I know him want to earn money by a proper job I understand that if he good environment for learning now or doing so be no bad, I try to help him learning English but not easy but I will direct that wa.... Should discover that what things he like or really want to do . oh dear my love I ..... your body so gentle, silken I thirst for touch, fondle your whole body get sex loo..... feeling oh god you make me crazy I love your body so soften it help easy to con... the attaching and mixture of our souls kisses you with much fire love I'm blessi... time must elapsing as quick as possible oh dear I thirst you so much now much Tuan

Love Letters from a Young Man | Antoinette de Morton

To: Anh Tuan
From: Antoinette De Morton

Dear God I hope your younger brother is not smoking heroin, it is so dangerous and addictive. We have many problems in Australia with heroin and so many young ones are wasting their lives and dying from overdoses. I can relate to your mother's .... Is very difficult when a woman has to work her whole life to bring up children whose husband is not there emotionally, physically and financially to help.

    I can honestly say my ex-husband has been a very good father to his children, a loving husband. Things change and he has a new woman who suits him, thinks like him so I can understand this and do not wish him ill. I just hope they work out things so no-one in our family will suffer from our marriage break-up and understand that in Vietnamese society it is very difficult for a woman to be with her husband and that appearances must be kept so as to not lose face. Naturally woman who ultimately suffers because here is no recourse for her to find a k... and to leave husband or get divorced. The husband does not care being he v.. have his needs met without really having to do anything to make life better for it sounds like your father needs a good kick up the arse, but I suppose he is a ... ways that he will never change. It is the worst thing for a father to lose the res... wife and children though maybe your father does not know or even understand. Maybe he is disillusioned with the way his life has turned out and no longer ca..

Date: Sunday 21 August 2005
Subject: My love
To: Antoinette De Morton
From: Anh Tuan

Hi my love you know I also have short span of time had dream in the noon 2 day ago we cuddled and tumble in the bed kisses with much fire and lippy in your lip spread out to your face look really lovely. I guess in my lip and around there also stick much lippy, I so happy with that in the dream, but when woke up little sad because you not here. My love I miss you so much your watch which you gave me still keep your perfume it's just waft but make me so crazy about you oh dear pictures as well, I thirst for you touching you, your pussy so cute soft your body also, kisses you my love, you with y whole heart. Tuan

---

To: Anh Tuan
From: Antoinette De Morton

I had a dream about you last night, that were together in this very unusual place full of colour and that we were entwined close and very peaceful, so I woke up very cheerful to a grey winter's day. I hope you are well. I miss you and the laughing that we have together, I am feeling a little lonely at night with just the cat to cuddle, my husband has got the message and no longer comes near me when he is here, which is not often these days. I have the house to myself pretty much at present so I have plenty of time to think and plan and make art. I can only plan in my head at the moment until things are resolved about the house. I have 2 exhibitions coming up though only group shows but this will keep me quite busy preparing work. I have not heard anymore from

Hong Kong as yet, these things take time. When I read your emails I feel that you are very ear me and I also long for your touch and caresses, my love, Antoinette.

Date: Wednesday 24 August 2005
Subject: I love you
To: Antoinette De Morton
From: Anh Tuan

Hi my love, the more I reading your emails is the more I love you and miss you so much the more I contacting to the people is the more I value respect and love you, the quicker elapsing of the time is the more I feel the time is stagnation (stop) I'm keen for you coming so much in order to prove for you that I love you by my whole heart and mind and I'm not intelligent but enough for understand that if has somebody deserve with the things which I've spent my value time my thought my heart my mind my sole is that person just be you no one else, I'm in earnest . and I also understand that you also love me much and you do so much things for me, I'm so appreciate that I don't know how to think you're less real . my love I miss you and love you so much kisses you, my love I want to say again that I really love Antoinette and miss so much. Tuan

---

To: Anh Tuan
From: Antoinette De Morton

I love the way you love me including my dark side, as you know there is no light without the dark we cannot see if there is no darkness to balance radiance and beauty, there can be no happiness if we do not understand some pain and hardship it means that when something wonderful happens we appreciate these things all the more. My life is becoming more confusing than ever with changes every day, sometimes I wonder how I even manage to see the light when at present life is very confronting with many things happening here. Now I am advised to see a lawyer and to get financial management with regard to my situation because my ex-husband is becoming a little difficult with arrangements. What I thought was amicable may prove not to be as clear cut. Anyway I will maintain and I am sure that things will resolve themselves in a good way, I am ever the optimist and naturally I am seeking all the advice that I can. I really do not think that things are different for women in any country with regard to rights, property etc albeit all women come from many different circumstances. My god in India they still burn women if a marriage goes sour so I am lucky in that I live in Australia and that I have many rights even though the man thinks not. It is my good fortune that I am educated and can access systems that are in place in this country, unfortunately though there are many women here who do not have enough English and go through hell because they cannot ask for help because they do not know how to go about such things. Maybe this is a role in life that I could take on to help uneducated and hardly done by women in different cultures, we will see. You send me such beautiful emails that my heart becomes full thinking of you. I hope that when I return to Hanoi that when we see each other again and you can see me really and still feel affection and love, things change so much and I am aware that you could come to idealise me in such a way that I become less real. I say this because I do understand many things and the vagaries of human nature, though I know your heart is pure and this is why we have connected in such a strong way. Forgive me if I write so much but miss our talking together and your constant questions, you always kept me thinking and my brain working even though I was in holiday la la land. Remember although a computer is less than poetic we at least can still communicate and you can say anything (which you have you little devil) I must say I certainly smile for sometime when I read your more racy emails though it makes it very difficult for me to sleep at night. All I know is that you are my darling and that I have your sweet face imprinted in my memory all my love Antoinette

Date: Friday 26 August 2005
Subject: Hello my darling
To: Antoinette De Morton
From: Anh Tuan

Hi my love I'm alright I miss you so much, seem the god always want to support me so he give me really nice people help me learning English so much I feel really appreciate about this that is a couple from Geelong of Australia, really nice people I really understanding for our situation, the more I knowing people is the more I love you and appreciate and value things which you reserve for me, you know now, I just say I thirst for your coming so much I'll hate myself if I make you feel have no fun with me because I love you so much I admit that I feel can not live without you my love I wish the time elapsing more quicker to December I miss your face every time you smile it's light of the sun make me feel warm and confidence to confront with the life, I love you and miss you so much kisses Antoinette. All of my heart for you. Antoinette

To: Anh Tuan
From: Antoinette De Morton

My love how are you? The time is going very quickly for me here and soon it will be December and I will get to see you. I am so looking forward to that moment I am still working on getting enough funds slowly but surely this is happening. It looks like I may be able to get the house I was talking to you about I am taking those issues day by day at the moment. I do hope however that things will be finalized by the end of the year. What have you been up to? Are you still talking to foreigners I the old quarter and met any interesting people. I would like to learn some Vietnamese, but my time is busy sorting out all these family issues and trying to meet deadlines with my art practice, hopefully I will have some spare time soon to maybe take classes. I miss you so much and just wish I could leave everything here and let everyone sort things out but this is not to be unfortunately. I do get a bit low with all the drama but I hve to hang in thee to get a final resolution. I am getting really horny, no sex is not good for me. I imagine you with me and near me so that helps but not quite the same as your actual presence. I have December to look forward to so that keeps me cheerful knowing that I will see you soon my love. Antoinette

Date:	Saturday 27 August 2005
Subject:	My love
To:	Antoinette De Morton
From:	Anh Tuan

Hi my love a day elapsed again and it means the more I miss you, it's bad when I can't sharing with you directly of everything I wish the time elapsing quick quicker. When I thought about the December I really feel ecstatic. Thank my love so much because your coming. Wish everything come smooth to you . my love you don't need to learn Vietnamese, it's waist of time when you come we learn it's ok, my love your image full in my mind you are so beautiful so cute when you cuddles me when you laughed and pat in my back said "deg man". I love it by now I miss you so much surge of your image come to my mind so cute so nice, kisses you love you so much Tuan.

Date: Sunday 28 August 2005
Subject: My love
To: Antoinette De Morton
From: Anh Tuan

Hi my love, I was born in Haiphong the north of Hanoi far away from Hanoi 100km. I came to Hanoi 11 years ago with my family, we moved because we met trouble in that city . during the time my mum was working in Haiphong she was chemical teacher in one of specialize high school in Haiphong she's been good teacher who get a lot of love respect from students because she is gentle understanding to students, their situation their taste .... but mostly teachers in Vietnam they don't care on the other hand, she had have good quality of teaching her subject nobody can refuse her about this point, she was issued a house before she got marriage, just two year later she born me, when I was eight years old the management of that school wanted to cut my house to the half in order to gave for another teacher in that school my mum have no choice she forced her self stand out and combated with them whole school (all of teachers just support the president of that school) even she wrong my mum so so frustrating protect every where, education service, municiple of that city but so hard for them because they just support people who have power, but my mum so persistent to protest. My love thanks so much when you want to hear my story I'm so appreciate of this kisses you love you so much Tuan.

I am so happy when you say like that, my love you know I love you so much. I understand myself is the most I'd never thought that will have someone love me like you I have nothing, really mediocre, only you value me from bottom of my heart I want say that I'm so lucky and I understand that luck not come two times in my live, I will do any thing in order to you never feel that you get mistake because you are together with me, or regret. I love you so much, some time I can explain but some time not, just one thing I'm sure that I love you from bottom of my heart about the renting don't worried i'll try the best. Much kisses my love I waiting to death for your coming love you so much Tuan.

I miss you too my sweet, I am madly trying to get the house clean and tidy for the real estate agent to come and have a look and give a quote. Things

are moving along slowly everyone here is a bit upset about having to sell the family home, but are gradually coming to terms with the idea. Change is always difficult but change can only bring new beginnings. I thought that after awhile you would forget about me and get on with your life in Vietnam. I am glad this is not so. When I come to Hanoi I am thinking of renting a small apartment so maybe you could help in finding out about prices. It maybe easier because you live in Hanoi and you can find out what is dodgy and what is not. I am looking at about $130-$200US a month if I get teaching work everything will be fine but I have to be prepared just in case this does not happen. My friends Mai Ho (born in Hanoi) and Penney Le Petite (an artist) will be in Hanoi from 20th January for a few weeks so that will be fun especially as it will be during Tet. Because of all the dramas here I have not had time to look into ticket prices but I will do so soon and let you now the outcome straight away. Everytime I email you I wish I was there with you I will kiss and love you to death when I come. Much love Antoinette.
   Anh Tuan

To: Anh Tuan
From: Antoinette De Morton

I have come home from a party with friends and a few red wines later hey here am I. I would love very much if you spoke to me about your life at present the day to day the small the large, your family, so I can learn more about you. I am being somewhat boring about my circumstances and I would love to find out so much about you, what you do each day how you are in your life, it is important that you share these things no matter what you think. I am interested in your whole life as a person and your dreams and schemes. How are all your friends I am interested too in their lives what concerns you what makes you happy nothing to do with me hey? Tell me everything even if you think it is not important, your mother, your father, your brother (how is he?) I can bring hairdressing things for him from here, hair dyes, etcetera anything he needs it is easy and not hard. P.S. I know how to do such things for women and men Colour Curl Straighten Dye all that women need and well cosmetics for all really. I also have my own German scissors for cutting hey all my friends love me they get free hair cuts, colour and champagne, while I look after them. No complaints yet, I am being somewhat frivolous but not too ha ha. If nothing else you have given me a gift for being constant in writing to you and writing how I feel about you and me also. It is an unusual place for me to be but I accept that this is so, I question everything and I get very nervous about the being of you and I. Because I live in my life, sometimes I worry that I am a fool to even consider that you my darling I love. This is of course me being rational and not emotional or romantic all of which I am. The one thing I know is that I care for you deeply an even though it seems strange in my day to day existence I will never not care for you. At this moment I feel silly and I wish that I can say and show everything that is in my heart. You are a young man with so much and I know this about you such passion, idealism, I will be there for you no matter what. Sometimes I am concerned that (I know I am an interesting and intelligent woman) that this could re arrange your concept of friends and family who will maybe find the notion of you and I strange, it certainly is here when I have explained, mostly my friends are whole hearted and happy and understand. I am still coming in December I consider you always. It is hard to explain I know I have a young heart but sometimes I forget and think of you and then realise that maybe somethings are so dumb. Remember you planted the kiss and then we had great sex my love but I am yours because I will never forget either. I am with you, all my love Antoinette

---

Date: Tuesday 30 August 2005
Subject: My darling
To: Antoinette De Morton
From: Anh Tuan

My love you know now I'm really want to be learning English in order achieve the top, I don't know why but really deep of my mind aspiring, I've been listening from ABC Pacific Channel and checking from dictionary (thanks you so much about the gift) afternoon I going around the lake to finding for talking, I will continue telling you about my story. My mum was called to many meetings just for question her about why she didn't give the half of this house but they ignore that my grandmother is mother of people who was died from the war it means he had merit for this country, it seem nothing important as power, you know it's one of big motive for me, sorry my love I must go now kisses you by most passionate I have, love you always by whole heart. Tuan

---

Date: Sunday 1 September 2005
Subject: I love you
To: Antoinette De Morton
From: Anh Tuan

Hi my love it's such so nice when you slap me I'd love to get that, ok love I will n... so much kisses you with the most passionate I have. Sorry little bit trouble with you soon.

Date:	Friday 2 September 2005
Subject:	I love you
To:	Antoinette De Morton
From:	Anh Tuan

Hi my love are you alright you know your ideas really subtle and profound it analyse somethings or express yourself you definitely right everythings in the balance but I just know really basic, I'll have a go to get to know the details, the source of water but I always thirst for that. My love you know yesterday ... order to talking to the people, I'm so surprise when has a foreigner girl want .... Working here in embassy she asked that if I have power what do I pay attention.... Ideas and she began introduce me bible she said much about the god (jehovah ... and the god like sculptor... general it's just basic one nothing relate to politics recommend me come to her home in Thursday night I order to learning more ... me more that class also have many Vietnamese as well I think her went to p... formula .. but any way I' really curious and keen to get to know that. My love. When looking at our pictures and remind the moment we got sex my penis ... but still suspending when that moment coming oh dear I'll give you crazy s... you so much Tuan.

Date: Sunday 4 September 2005
Subject: I love you
To: Anh Tuan
From: Antoinette De Morton

I love you too, you are so cute and of course you think about sex a lot, so do I as I go to be (with the cat) I am getting used to this situation but it does not mean ... day brings a new challenge and I am sure this is meant to be for me to understand things move at their own momentum, things that I have no c.... always understood these things and am re learning to just be in some ways and this reality. I can have some input to the best of my capacity but things sometimes ... Do not say to me again about stupid remember I say I slap you ha ha. this is the formula for life nothing opposite interestingly enough, life/death, humour/sadness, happiness/pain, life paradoxical notions and change the only constant. As I said to you I have never had many words to anybody but you, for some reason you bring out something in me, some way to the vagaries of life. I remember you said I was too trusting, well my .. that I will be hurt but I do not believe these things. My husband is not a bad man .. then I hve been foolish too. It takes two people to break a marriage and unfortunately mended again. Many people put up with difficult situations because they th ...

am a free spirit and about now I am willing to embrace everything that will unfold .. thinking is not so bad it is part of my artistic life and when I make art people like which as I said was how I got to be back in Hanoi when we met and of course I ha ha. You are my darling so please never say stupid to me again, if you were …. Person you are we would not be writing or having great sex (it seems a long wh....

Date: Thursday 8 September 2005
Subject: I love you
To: Antoinette De Morton
From: Anh Tuan

Hi my love how are you now, I understand why you said that you re in your …. mine like last email I said it's really logical in my mind you are only one person .. valuable and respect me and love me I now that thinking not come easy from also respect yours, so gentle, tolerant for every body even that man so bad b…good point from them for tolerant aways pen mind for learning observing, th… much emotion .. you know all of that points definitely resemble with me I'm de…. Because I know I'm stupid and must learning, absorbing from everyone so I … person like you especially is the girl just come to me one time in my life it's real love you with my pragmatical thinking and of course I also love you other way body your characteristic your stylc your gesture … of course your crazy thinking love, love you so much Tuan.

Date:	Thursday 8 September 2005
Subject:	I love you
To:	Anh Tuan
From:	Antoinette De Morton

My dear darling I would never upset you for the world. When I said about the fun I have crazy sense of humour as you know. I just think in a different way and when my friend showed me some things I thought hey great and that I .. your gorgeous person in these things I know it sounds strange from where here things are different as I know and it is hard in some ways to reconcile understand about you, so please do not misunderstand. I remember when ..... gave you a shirt and you liked it so much so because I remember this I tho... get you designer label hey hey !!!! from my friend who is gifted by the way w... and designing and will do anything for me anyhow because he is a good friend.. the hell my sweet I am a romantic as I have said and I can picture you in al.. physically "I wish" and mentally this of course has to keep me entertained u... again, so I think in arbitrary ways sometimes that comes from my culture and will get my friend to keep his word as he did say he would love to make some ... would be seen in Hanoi by somebody who could wear such things so there fact he wishes that when I come to Hanoi I can find things for him for in... unusual art things posters etc. he is a very avant guarde kind of designer and interested in any things. As you know I am an artist and open to all conce... endeavour good and bad because it is all these complexities that make us and I, you, young and me a fully fledged woman albeit with wings that still t.. bird newly hatched wings aspread gliding into the universe. Life no matter what can full of so many things some of which we understand and most of which thought that at this stage of my life I would know much but I am like a child like you thirsting for more knowledge it is a strange thing to be met at this m.... knowing that you care about me and love me, you are so young and so beautiful, some ways I can not comprehend your feelings for me. When I am in my ra ... think everything is insane and yet I treasure your every thought and email a... everything for you, my love, caring and all my thoughts ae with you. It is h..... am here in my reality and you are with yours and I wonder and wonder how so.

You are my dear darling and I love you Antoinette

Thanks my love I understood that but I just wonder about politic, I trust my self de ... American they want to imbue Vietnamese about politic under the religious form .. know it's so denger because the Vietnamese government afraid of religious because .. and I understand that you love me so I definitely not involve in Jehovah love you ...

To: Anh Tuan
From: Antoinette De Morton

My dear love, while the love of god is in this person's heart it is a form of cult indoctrination please with all my love run a mile or several. I know it can only be about you not a force (Jehovah's Witness come from America and send young .. to their church) they come to Australia and it is their mission to convert to any converted there becomes no freedom of speech or thinking other than what this heart I beg you not to go there, it seems seductive at first but is the antithesis and you have this in abundance for many things if you get caught in a rigid w..... you strive against. I can only suggest to you the things that I am aware about brain go birko ha ha, particularly Jehovah's Witness. This group come from m... From my point of you it is your decision how you deal with this situation all I am caution. Also, they are not into sex or fun or anything that much and our situation believe in life and humans and their capacity for beauty, goodness and god th..... beliefs and this is true freedom not to be told what is good for us, to question understanding of what is true and what is not. When another ideology impinging me for this strong email if we were together I could discuss with you more col... me I will not let you down I know everything changes you are open to so much be my gift to you from the universe, you are so intelligent and because I unde.... Sent on a journey that is not about you. When you met me you judged right yo.... understand, as I said no matter what you talk to me about anything. One of the ... without judgement (not too much ha ha) love beauty and people who are always least he is real he will put you straight re: Jehovah's Witness, please give him Hanoi and rave him up a little he will understand. I am really good I know I th.... Expect? No other woman in the universe would do what I am doing ha. ha. lo..... involved with Jehovah's. Antoinette

PPS I love you permanent erection sou ..... that so much ha ha.

www.ingramcontent.com/pod-product-compliance
Lightning Source LLC
Chambersburg PA
CBHW041145110526
44590CB00027B/4127